Original title:
Prosperous Life

Copyright © 2024 Creative Arts Management OÜ
All rights reserved.

Author: Thor Castlebury
ISBN HARDBACK: 978-9916-88-550-5
ISBN PAPERBACK: 978-9916-88-551-2

Tranquility in Growth

In silent woods where shadows play,
The gentle breeze whispers the day.
Life awakens in tender hues,
Embracing dawn with hopeful views.

Roots stretch deep in the fertile ground,
Where hidden strength can soon be found.
Each leaf unfurls in morning light,
A symphony of green so bright.

Time flows softly like a stream,
Nurturing every tender dream.
The earth sings songs of quiet grace,
Inviting all to find their place.

In every branch and every bud,
Lies a promise, a quiet thud.
With patience, nature's dance unfolds,
A tale of life that never grows old.

The Garden of Aspirations

In the garden where dreams bloom,
Whispers of hope find their room.
Petals of courage, soft and bright,
Guiding the heart toward the light.

Beneath the shade of ancient trees,
Fluttering leaves dance in the breeze.
Seeds of desire scattered wide,
Nurtured by faith, they won't hide.

With each dawn, the blossoms grow,
Fertile soil where wishes flow.
The fragrance of goals fills the air,
In this haven, we find our care.

In the twilight, visions rest,
Cradled close in nature's quest.
The stars above grant us a sign,
In this garden, our spirits shine.

Echoes of Radiance

In the silence, whispers play,
Echoes of light lead the way.
Shadows soft against the wall,
In this moment, we hear the call.

The sun dips low, a golden hue,
Painting skies in vibrant blue.
Every flicker, a story told,
Illuminates hearts, brave and bold.

From dusk till dawn, the dance unfolds,
Fragments of warmth in our souls.
With every pulse, the night ignites,
Igniting dreams in starry heights.

Here in shadows, we find our grace,
Reflections of love we can embrace.
In the echoes, we find our stance,
A radiant song, a living dance.

Waves of Fortune

Upon the shore, the tides embrace,
Waves of fortune, a gentle race.
They weave their tales in fluid lines,
Guided by fate, the heart aligns.

In the depths, treasures await,
Whispers of hope, a fervent state.
With each surf, a chance to seize,
The rhythm of life flows with ease.

Sails unfurled to chase the breeze,
Navigating dreams with grace and ease.
Fortunes come, like the sea's caress,
In the flow, we find our success.

As the sun sets, all is clear,
In the waves, we conquer fear.
United with nature's call to roam,
In this vast ocean, we find our home.

The Dawn of Plenty

In the horizon, light breaks free,
A dawn of plenty, wild and free.
Colors splash across the sky,
Awakening hopes that never die.

With morning's touch, the world does rise,
Golden fields under brightening skies.
Fruits of labor, rich and bold,
Harvested dreams, a tale retold.

Songs of joy fill the air,
In every heart, abundance shared.
With gratitude, we greet the day,
In the dawn's glow, we find our way.

As sunlight beckons, we stand tall,
Embracing life, we heed the call.
In the dawn of plenty, we rejoice,
In every heartbeat, we find our voice.

Pathways of Plenty

In fields of gold where blessings grow,
The sunbeams dance, a warm, soft glow.
With every step, a dream unfolds,
A tale of abundance, timeless and bold.

Rivers of fortune carve the way,
Winding through life, come what may.
Each choice a seed, each moment a chance,
To rise with the dawn in a joyous dance.

Whispers of the Wealthy

In chambers deep where secrets lie,
The hushed tones of the affluent sigh.
Their laughter echoes through gilded halls,
Yet wisdom whispers in silent calls.

What worth is gold if hearts turn cold?
In lonely splendor, stories unfold.
True riches bloom in kindness shared,
A legacy crafted, a world to be spared.

The Art of Living Well

In simple moments, joy is found,
A cup of tea, the laughter around.
Beneath the moon's soft silver light,
Life's art is painted in colors bright.

With every breath, a treasure untold,
In connection deep, we forge the gold.
To cherish time and embrace the now,
Is the masterpiece we create with a vow.

Luminous Echoes

In a world awash with vibrant hues,
Each voice a star, each heart a muse.
Echoes of laughter weave a bright thread,
In unity's glow, we move ahead.

Through shadows dark, a beacon shines,
Hopeful whispers cross the lines.
With every dream that dares to rise,
We create a symphony beneath the skies.

Kaleidoscope of Abundance

In fields where flowers bloom and sway,
Colors dance in bright array.
Joyful whispers fill the air,
Life's a canvas, bold and rare.

Golden grains beneath the sun,
Harvest dreams, for all, not one.
Every heartbeat, every sound,
Nature's gifts, so rich, profound.

In gentle rains and shining beams,
Hope awakens, fuels our dreams.
The world spins in vibrant hues,
A symphony of varied views.

Together we embrace the light,
Sharing blessings, futures bright.
In this kaleidoscope we find,
Abundance shared, heart entwined.

Crowned in Colors

Veils of violet wrap the dawn,
As new horizons draw us on.
In the garden where we play,
Nature's crown, in bright display.

Scarlet petals kiss the breeze,
Golden sun through verdant trees.
Every color tells a tale,
In this world, we shall prevail.

From azure skies to emerald fields,
The palette of life, love, it yields.
Hand in hand, we carve our way,
Crowned in colors, bold, we stay.

Whispers of the wind are sweet,
Promises of hope we greet.
In this tapestry of grace,
Together we embrace our place.

A Tapestry Woven

Threads of silver, gold, and blue,
Weaving dreams in every hue.
In unity, our stories twine,
A tapestry, yours and mine.

Each moment stitched with love and care,
In every knot, a thought to share.
Binding heart to heart, we see,
In this fabric, we are free.

Colors blend in harmony,
Forming shapes of destiny.
With every twist, a vision grows,
In this weaving, life bestows.

Through trials faced and joys unfurled,
Together, we can change the world.
In the looms of time, we stand,
A tapestry, hand in hand.

The Blossoming Spirit

From the soil, we draw our strength,
In the garden of life, great lengths.
Roots run deep, gathering light,
Together, we embrace our flight.

Petals open, colors bright,
Awakening with pure delight.
In the dance of sun and rain,
Love's reflection breaks the chain.

Each breath a promise, softly spoken,
In the silence, hearts unbroken.
From bud to bloom, we rise anew,
The spirit blossoms, pure and true.

With every season, we renew,
In the embrace of skies so blue.
Together, we will ever grow,
In the garden, love will flow.

Bright Horizons

Golden rays break through the night,
Chasing shadows, bringing light.
Hope unfurls with every dawn,
In the silence, dreams are drawn.

Fields adorned with colors bright,
Nature's canvas, pure delight.
With every step, a journey starts,
Together we mend our hearts.

United in Growth

Seeds of change we plant today,
In unity, we find our way.
Roots entangled, strong and deep,
In this bond, our dreams we keep.

As we nurture, watch us rise,
Reaching upward towards the skies.
Hand in hand, we break the mold,
In our growth, a tale unfolds.

The Dance of Flourishing Hearts

In rhythm, hearts find their beat,
A waltz of joy, a bond so sweet.
With every twirl, we understand,
Together strong, we take a stand.

Petals sway in gentle breeze,
Whispers shared among the trees.
With laughter bright and spirits free,
We dance through life, you and me.

The Joyful Tides

Waves come crashing on the shore,
Each new moment, there's so much more.
Laughter dances on the sea,
In these tides, we're wild and free.

As the sun dips low and shy,
Colors blend across the sky.
Together we embrace the phase,
In joyful tides, we spend our days.

Echoes of Plenty

In fields where golden grains do sway,
Chasing the warm, bright sun's soft ray,
Whispers of harvest fill the air,
Nature's bounty, beyond compare.

The rivers dance, the hills stand tall,
Echoes of laughter, a joyful call,
Fruits of labor ripe and sweet,
Gathering joy with each heartbeat.

Underneath the starlit night,
Crops of hope bathed in moonlight,
Each seed sewn with dreams untold,
In these echoes, wealth unfolds.

With grateful hearts, we lift our song,
For in this land, we all belong,
Echoes of plenty, a vibrant cheer,
Together we stand, year after year.

The Thriving Soul

A flicker of fire within the chest,
Awakens the dreamer, on a quest,
With each sunrise, new passions bloom,
In boundless spaces, hearts find room.

The road is long, yet spirits soar,
With every step, we long for more,
Through valleys deep and mountains wide,
The thriving soul becomes our guide.

With friendships forged in laughter's light,
And visions dancing in the night,
We chase the stars, embracing grace,
In the thriving soul, we find our place.

Each moment lived, a vibrant tome,
In unity, we find our home,
A tapestry woven with dreams and love,
A soaring anthem, like the dove.

Oasis of Dreams

In the desert's heart, a secret lies,
An oasis blooms beneath the skies,
With whispers sweet and waters clear,
A sanctuary where spirits steer.

Palm fronds sway in the gentle breeze,
Nature's embrace, a perfect ease,
Where visions glow like the morning sun,
In this refuge, all worries shun.

With laughter ringing through golden sands,
Hope awakens in tender hands,
A tapestry of dreams unfurled,
In the oasis, a vibrant world.

Together we wander, hand in hand,
Creating a life, so well planned,
In the quiet whispers of this place,
Lives a promise, wrapped in grace.

A Symphony of Plenty

Strings of laughter fill the air,
In melodies sweet, we find our care,
Harmony blooms in every heart,
A symphony where dreams take part.

Each note we play, a story spun,
In time with nature, we're all one,
With rhythm flowing, our spirits rise,
Under the vast and endless skies.

Wind and waves in perfect sync,
Artistry blooms, inviting us to think,
About the beauty, pure and bright,
In a symphony that sings of light.

Together we dance, our souls entwined,
In this abundance, love defined,
A symphony of plenty, strong and true,
An endless promise, ever new.

Vibrant Landscapes Ahead

Fields of green stretch far and wide,
Mountains touch the endless blue,
Rivers dance with gentle pride,
Nature whispers secrets new.

Sunsets blaze in colors bright,
Stars awaken in the night,
Paths unfold with every step,
Promise lingers, dreams adept.

Whispers of the morning dew,
Petals glisten, fresh and bold,
Every shade a vibrant hue,
Stories of the earth retold.

In this landscape, hearts take flight,
Joyful souls in pure delight,
Embrace the beauty, breathe it in,
Vibrant places where we begin.

Illuminated by Gratitude

In the dawn of a new day,
Hearts embrace the warmth of light,
Every moment, bright as May,
Gratitude makes burdens light.

Whispers of a thankful song,
Echoes in the gentle air,
Holding tight where souls belong,
Love and kindness everywhere.

Each small kindness, like a spark,
Lighting paths that seem so dark,
With each step, we find our way,
Illuminated by each day.

In the circle of our friends,
Gratitude never truly ends,
Health, and love, and laughter shared,
In this light, together we dared.

Echoes of Generosity

Hands extended, hearts aligned,
Gifts of love in every shape,
Echoes of a spirit kind,
In this world, we all escape.

Sharing burdens, lifting souls,
With each act, we sow a seed,
Generosity makes us whole,
In our hearts, a deeper creed.

Ripples flow from every deed,
Touching lives in unseen ways,
In giving, we fulfill a need,
Echoes linger, bright as rays.

Together, we shall stand and grow,
In our hearts, a steady glow,
Creating futures, bold and free,
Echoes of our unity.

The Heart's Jackpot

In the depths of tender hearts,
Love's a treasure, rich and rare,
Each soft whisper gently starts,
To reveal what we all share.

Moments shared in quiet grace,
Laughter ringing, pure delight,
Every smile a warm embrace,
Gold that glimmers in the night.

Kindred spirits, side by side,
In this game of life we play,
Winning with a love that's wide,
Finding joy in every day.

With each step, the heart, it grows,
Harvesting what true love sows,
In life's game, we hold the key,
The heart's jackpot, you and me.

Circles of Light

Upon the dawn, the shadows flee,
A golden glow sets spirits free.
Whispers of hope in the warm embrace,
The world awakens with gentle grace.

In every heart, a flame ignites,
Dancing like stars on tranquil nights.
Together we weave, a radiant sight,
In the boundless circles of light.

Through fields of dreams, we wander bright,
Chasing the sun, from morn till night.
Each step we take, a path unique,
In the quiet glow, the soul will speak.

Hand in hand, through joy and strife,
We cherish the beauty of this life.
In the tapestry spun, we find our right,
A journey shared, in circles of light.

The Dance of Dreams

In twilight's gleam, we find our way,
Where shadows play and spirits sway.
With every heartbeat, we shall rise,
Embracing the magic that never dies.

The moonbeams whisper, secrets unfold,
Promises of wonders yet untold.
In the realm where wishes gleam,
Together we waltz in the dance of dreams.

Through skies of color, we take our flight,
A symphony woven with stars so bright.
With laughter and love, our souls entwine,
In this night's embrace, your heart is mine.

As dawn approaches, we twirl in light,
Grateful for every shared delight.
In every moment, we dare to scheme,
Forever lost in the dance of dreams.

A Harvest of Hearts

In fields of gold, we gather time,
Each moment ripe, a gift so prime.
With hands outstretched, we weave the art,
Of love and laughter, a harvest of hearts.

The sun bestows its warm caress,
On paths of joy, we feel the blessed.
With every smile, a seed we sow,
In the garden where friendship grows.

Through seasons change, we hold the thread,
Of shared stories, both spoken and read.
United we stand, never apart,
Collecting memories, a harvest of hearts.

In the twilight glow, we celebrate,
All that we've nurtured, never too late.
Together we flourish, love's gentle chart,
In every embrace, a harvest of hearts.

The Elixir of Existence

In every droplet, life unfolds,
An elixir of stories, both new and old.
With every breath, a chance to find,
The essence of life within the mind.

Through trials faced, we learn to grow,
In the depths of pain, wisdom will flow.
With open hearts, we dare to grieve,
In the journey's weave, we learn to believe.

The stars above, they light our path,
With laughter and love to shield the wrath.
In the whispers of time, we find our bliss,
In the elixir of existence's kiss.

So raise a glass to all we share,
In this wild ride, beyond compare.
Together we sip, with grateful hearts,
The elixir of existence, as life imparts.

Pathways of Promise

In the morning's gentle light,
Footsteps trace a hopeful way.
Each step whispers dreams in flight,
Guiding us to a brighter day.

Beneath the boughs of ancient trees,
Where shadows dance and secrets hide.
We find the strength in whispered pleas,
And trust the path that we decide.

With every turn, new visions grow,
Revealing paths yet unexplored.
Through trials faced and seeds we sow,
The journey's worth, our spirit's sword.

So let us walk, hand in hand,
Through valleys low and mountains high.
In unity, we take a stand,
For in this bond, no dreams can die.

The Richness of Each Breath

A breath, a pause, in life's embrace,
Inhale the world, exhale the doubt.
Each moment counts, a sacred space,
In silence, hear the heart's own shout.

With every breath, we touch the sky,
Feel life's pulse in every sigh.
A tapestry of joys we weave,
In mindfulness, we learn to believe.

In chaos found, a calm retreat,
The richness of this breath reveals.
In every heartbeat, life's own beat,
Awakening all that love conceals.

So cherish this, our gift so grand,
With open hearts, let wonder flow.
In every breath, a life well-planned,
As gratitude begins to grow.

Whispers of Wealth

In a garden filled with grace,
We gather treasures from the ground.
Each blossom tells its own sweet place,
In whispers soft, our joy is found.

Wealth is not just gold or stone,
But laughter shared and kindness sown.
In moments spent with those we love,
True riches grow, as stars above.

With every smile, a spark ignites,
With every touch, a world unfolds.
Life's simple joys, our guiding lights,
In whispers sweet, our tale is told.

So count these blessings, small yet bright,
In every heart, the wealth we wield.
Together we shall shine our light,
In gratitude, our dreams revealed.

Spirals of Ascendancy

Upwards we climb, through tangled vines,
A dance with fate, each twist a chance.
In every challenge, strength defines,
As determination spurs the prance.

With courage held, we forge ahead,
Each spiral taking us anew.
In heights of hope, our spirits fed,
We learn to trust and to renew.

With eyes on stars, we aim for more,
Embracing life's expansive view.
In every leap, we softly soar,
Creating paths in skies so blue.

So let us rise, in unison,
Through storms that challenge and subdue.
In unity, all fears outrun,
Together, we will see it through.

Bounty Beneath the Skies

Fields of green stretch wide and far,
Golden grains beneath the sun.
Nature's gifts, a shining star,
Harvesting joy for everyone.

Trees adorned with fruits so bright,
Beneath their boughs, the laughter flows.
In the warm and soft twilight,
Life's abundance gently grows.

Clouds drift softly, dreams take flight,
Every breeze sings songs of cheer.
In this bounty, hearts ignite,
Together we find love so near.

Seasons change, yet truths remain,
Through every storm, we find our way.
In nature's hand, we hold no pain,
Beneath the skies, we choose to stay.

Radiance in Each Step

With every stride, the world awakes,
Footsteps dance on paths of gold.
Every moment, a chance it makes,
Stories of life, waiting to unfold.

The sun breaks through the misty air,
Illuminating dreams we chase.
With hearts alight, we choose to care,
In each breath, we find our place.

The whispers of the winding road,
Guide us on through dark and light.
In our journey, love's the code,
Radiant souls, shining bright.

Together we embrace the road,
Hand in hand, through thick and thin.
In every sunbeam, hope bestowed,
With radiance, our hearts will win.

Sowing Joy

In gardens green, we plant our dreams,
Seeds of laughter, blooms of love.
Nurturing hope, as sunlight beams,
In every heart, the joy we shove.

Hands in the earth, a sacred touch,
Watered with kindness, powered by care.
With every gesture, we create much,
A tapestry of joy we share.

As blossoms rise, so do our souls,
In vibrant colors, life unfolds.
Together, we achieve our goals,
Sowing seeds of joy, pure and bold.

Through seasons' change, our spirits grow,
In unity, we'll reap the bliss.
In every heart, let kindness flow,
Sowing joy in every kiss.

Illuminated Journeys

In twilight hours, paths are seen,
With every step, a flame ignites.
Guided by stars and love's serene,
    We discover new delights.

The road ahead may twist and turn,
But in our hearts, a glow remains.
With every lesson, new we learn,
    Illuminated by joy's refrains.

Through mountains high and valleys low,
    We carry light, with courage sure.
Each journey lasts, as we all know,
    A testament that we endure.

Together, we will always roam,
Hand in hand, through night and day.
On illuminated paths we comb,
With every step, we find our way.

Streams of Hope

In the valley where dreams flow,
Soft whispers of the past go.
Nature's grace in gentle tides,
Where the heart forever abides.

Mirrors of the sky above,
Reflecting pure and tender love.
Each ripple sings a quiet song,
Guiding souls as they move along.

Amid the rocks and emerald weeds,
Life awakens, and sorrow bleeds.
Hope springs eternal in the air,
A promise whispered everywhere.

In those streams of crystal light,
Shadows fade, and hearts take flight.
With every drop, a chance to live,
The waters flow, and love will give.

A Garden of Dreams

In the garden, colors bloom,
Fragrant petals chase the gloom.
Whispers dance in morning dew,
Each flower tells a tale anew.

Beneath the arch of emerald leaves,
Heartfelt secrets the garden weaves.
The sunbeams kiss the earth with grace,
As shadows twirl, and moments trace.

Butterflies in joyous flight,
Flitting 'neath the stars' soft light.
In this haven, souls unite,
A tapestry of pure delight.

Every seed a wish begun,
In the garden where hearts run.
Fostering a world of peace,
With nature's touch, all worries cease.

Treasures Beneath the Surface

Beneath the waves, where secrets lie,
Whispers of the ocean sigh.
Pearls of wisdom, soft and bright,
Waiting to be found by light.

Tides that ebb and flow with grace,
Guarding treasures in their space.
Fragments of a world unseen,
Of ancient songs and places dreamed.

In the depths, where shadows play,
Mysteries unfold by day.
Eager hearts dive deep and bold,
To uncover stories long untold.

Gems of time in water's hold,
Lessons learned, and fears consoled.
As the sea reveals its worth,
We find our place upon this Earth.

Flourishing Winds

Softly blowing, gentle air,
Whispers brush away our care.
In the trees, the branches sway,
Healing hearts in nature's play.

Wind that carries dreams afar,
Guides the soul like a bright star.
With each gust, a chance to soar,
Letting go, we find our core.

In the dance of leaves and sky,
Hope can rise and fears comply.
Through every cycle, life renews,
Flourishing winds, fanning our views.

Embrace the currents, wild and free,
Let them lead you, come and see.
In the winds, our spirits blend,
Lifelong journeys never end.

The Bounty of Tomorrow

Hope blooms in the dawn's soft light,
Dreams take flight, chasing the night.
Fields of gold in the morning's hue,
A promise made for me and you.

Paths we wander, hand in hand,
Together we rise, together we stand.
With every step, new joys unfold,
The future's treasure, worth more than gold.

Seas may roar and winds may scream,
Yet we find peace in our shared dream.
Harvests gathered from kindness sown,
In the garden of hope we have grown.

As stars align in the evening sky,
We chase the dreams that never die.
The bounty of tomorrow awaits our turn,
In every heart, a fire to burn.

Wealth of the Heart

Love's gentle whispers weave through sighs,
In every glance, the soul complies.
Riches found in laughter shared,
In simple moments, love declared.

Hands entwined on a winter's night,
Warmth within, an endless light.
Gold may fade, and treasures fall,
But the wealth of hearts transcends it all.

Memories cherished like ageless wine,
In the tapestry of life, we divine.
Through trials faced and joys embraced,
In the depths of love, true wealth replaced.

In kindness given, in words sincere,
The wealth of the heart, forever near.
With love's embrace, we stand apart,
Rich beyond measure, our guiding chart.

Sunlit Journeys

Paths unfold in the morning glare,
With sunlit dreams adrift in air.
In golden fields where shadows play,
We wander free, come what may.

The laughter of streams beneath the sun,
In every step, our hearts are one.
Mountains high and valleys wide,
In nature's arms, we find our guide.

Colors dance as the day will fade,
In twilight's glow, plans are laid.
Each moment lived is a gift divine,
In sunlit journeys, our spirits shine.

With every dawn, new trails will call,
Together we'll rise and never fall.
Adventures await, with skies so clear,
In sunlit journeys, we find our cheer.

The Dance of Abundance

Life is a waltz on a vibrant stage,
With steps of joy, we turn the page.
In every spin and every leap,
The dance of abundance our souls keep.

A symphony of laughter fills the air,
In the rhythm of love, we find our flair.
Hands raised high, we join the song,
In the dance of abundance, we all belong.

The twirling stars in the velvet night,
Guide our hearts in pure delight.
With every heartbeat, a story unfolds,
In the dance of life, we are bold.

So let us sway in this grand ballet,
Celebrate abundance in every way.
With joy as our guide, we take a chance,
Together we'll weave the eternal dance.

Seeds of Serenity

In quiet fields where whispers grow,
The seeds of peace begin to sow.
They dance beneath the gentle sun,
And cradle dreams when day is done.

A breeze that flows, so calm, so light,
Carries the hopes into the night.
Each petal soft, a story told,
Of lives embraced, of hearts consoled.

Time's gentle touch, a rhythm sweet,
Guides every soul in soft retreat.
Together, we shall find our place,
In nature's arms, a warm embrace.

With every dawn, a promise made,
To nurture love and bloom, not fade.
In seeds of serenity, we find,
A garden grown for heart and mind.

Fortunes in the Folds

Amidst the creases, stories lie,
Of hopes and dreams that dare to fly.
Each twist and turn, a chance to see,
The fortune found, the mystery.

In every fold, a whisper waits,
Of joy, of grief, of fragile fates.
Unraveled truths beneath the seams,
The tapestry of all our dreams.

A hidden path, a secret lane,
Where laughter dances free from pain.
The riches gained in silent trust,
Are worth their weight in gold and dust.

So gather close, and share the gold,
In every story, young and old.
For fortunes lie within our hearts,
In every fold, a world departs.

The Tapestry of Riches

Threads of color weave a tale,
Of every journey, every trail.
In patterns bold, our lives connect,
A tapestry of rich effect.

Each stitch a moment, vibrant, bright,
A testament to day and night.
Together stitched in joy and sorrow,
A legacy for each tomorrow.

From humble threads to golden hue,
Each heart contributes, tried and true.
A work of art, a shared embrace,
In unity, we find our place.

So let us gather, let us weave,
In kindness shown, we will believe.
The tapestry, our stories blend,
A cloth of richness without end.

Radiant Horizons

Beyond the hills, where sunlight glows,
A promise waits, a chance to grow.
With every dawn, new colors rise,
Painting dreams across the skies.

The gentle breeze, a call to roam,
Inviting us to find our home.
In every shade, a future bright,
Guiding us through the endless night.

With every step, the world unfolds,
New adventures found, new stories told.
The horizon gleams, a radiant guide,
In courage born, we shall abide.

So lift your gaze, embrace the glow,
For in this journey, love will flow.
Radiant horizons, forever near,
In every heartbeat, chase the clear.

Dreams Unfolding

In the quiet of the night,
Stars above shine so bright.
Whispers of hope take flight,
As dreams begin to ignite.

With each thought, visions weave,
Patterns of what we believe.
In the heart, secrets cleave,
Awakening what we conceive.

Paths of color and light,
Guide us through shadows and fright.
In the dawn, we find our sight,
As dreams unfold, pure and right.

Together, we'll embrace,
Every challenge we will face.
With each pulse, we'll find our place,
In a world of endless grace.

Wealth in Experience

Through valleys deep and wide,
Life's lessons coincide.
Every stumble, every stride,
Richness in time we bide.

A treasure forged in pain,
Moments lost and regained.
In the sunshine and the rain,
Wisdom's gem we attain.

Stories etched in the soul,
Fragments that make us whole.
In the dance, we find our role,
Life's beauty takes its toll.

Cherishing years as they pass,
Each memory a piece of glass.
Shining bright in time's vast mass,
Wealth in experience will amass.

The Song of Possibilities

In the morning light we rise,
With hope dancing in our eyes.
Endless choices fill the skies,
A melody that never dies.

Voices of dreams intertwined,
In every heart, paths we find.
New adventures, unconfined,
The song of life, lovingly rhymed.

Futures bright as stars align,
Every moment, a design.
With courage, our spirits shine,
Creating stories, yours and mine.

So let us sing, let us soar,
Open windows, swing wide the door.
In the symphony, we'll explore,
The song of possibilities, forevermore.

Nurtured by Nature

In the forest's gentle embrace,
Life unfolds at its own pace.
Whispers of wind we trace,
In nature, we find our place.

Mountains rise, horizons wide,
With rivers that flow with pride.
In every creature, love resides,
Nature's beauty is our guide.

Every petal, every leaf,
Breathes a story, brings relief.
In solitude or with belief,
Nurtured by nature, we find peace.

So let us wander, let us roam,
Amongst the trees, we feel at home.
Nature's arms, our heart's sweet comb,
In her presence, love will bloom.

The Symphony of Success

A melody of dreams takes flight,
With each note playing bold and bright.
Through trials faced, we find our way,
Success awaits at break of day.

With harmony, we stand as one,
Together 'til the day is done.
The rhythm of our hearts aligns,
In every beat, ambition shines.

Each challenge met, a song we sing,
In unity, our spirits cling.
The symphony of life will play,
As we embrace a brand new day.

Nestled in Plenty

In fields of green, the treasures lie,
Each grain of hope, beneath the sky.
Nestled in plenty, hearts will bloom,
In every corner, joy will loom.

The sun will shine on dreams anew,
As love unfolds, and skies turn blue.
In abundance, we find our peace,
Through every moment, joys increase.

Together we'll cultivate our land,
With gentle hands, we'll take a stand.
In every seed, a story grows,
Nestled in plenty, life bestows.

Wings of Fulfillment

With wings outstretched, we rise and soar,
In search of dreams we've longed for more.
The heights we reach, through skies so wide,
In every moment, we take pride.

Our hearts are free, like birds in flight,
Chasing the stars beneath the night.
With every flutter, we embrace,
The winds of change, a bold new space.

Through valleys deep and mountains high,
We'll journey forth, our spirits nigh.
With wings of hope, we find our way,
In pursuit of joy, come what may.

The Alchemy of Joy

In every tear, a lesson learned,
With every laughter, warmth returned.
The alchemy of joy ignites,
Transforming shadows into lights.

Through every trial, our hearts grow strong,
In unity, we find belong.
With threads of gold, we weave our tale,
In the face of winds, we shall not pale.

In nature's arms, we find our bliss,
Each moment cherished, none amiss.
The magic flows in all we do,
The alchemy of joy shines true.

Golden Threads of Tomorrow

In the dawn's embrace, we weave our dreams,
Golden threads of hope in sunlight beams.
Each wish a promise, strong and bright,
Guiding our path through day and night.

With every step, the future unfolds,
A tapestry of stories, rich and bold.
The whispers of destiny softly call,
Together we'll rise, we will not fall.

Hand in hand, we'll brave the storm,
Transforming shadows into warmth.
In unity, we find our strength,
A journey measured in heart and length.

Tomorrow awaits, a canvas anew,
With colors of dreams, both bright and true.
We stitch our fate with love and grace,
In golden threads, we find our place.

Flourishing Paths

Winding roads beneath the sun,
Every step leads to places fun.
Through fields of flowers, vibrant and wide,
Nature's beauty, our joyful guide.

The rustle of leaves, the chirp of birds,
Reminds us to pause, to speak in words.
About the wonders that life can bring,
In the heart of nature, we spread our wings.

With each turn, new sights to see,
The paths unfold, wild and free.
In laughter and love, our spirits soar,
Life's journey together, forevermore.

As twilight descends, stars take flight,
We cherish the moments, soft and bright.
In every shadow, light still beams,
Flourishing paths lead to our dreams.

Seeds of Serendipity

In the garden of chance, we plant our seeds,
Whispers of fortune, fulfilling our needs.
Sprouting with joy, these gifts of fate,
Nature's surprises, never too late.

With laughter and love, the blooms arise,
Petals of happiness, a sweet surprise.
Through storms and sun, they learn to grow,
Resilience found in each ebb and flow.

Every chance encounter, a spark ignites,
Connections blossom, igniting lights.
In fleeting moments, magic we find,
Serendipity weaving, gently entwined.

So nurture your dreams, let them take flight,
In the soil of hope, they'll reach their height.
Together we'll cherish this beautiful spree,
For life is a dance of serendipity.

The Wealth of Moments

In fleeting seconds, treasures reside,
Time whispers softly, a gentle guide.
Collecting smiles, we weave our tale,
In the tapestry of life, we cannot fail.

The laughter of friends, a warm embrace,
Moments of joy, time cannot replace.
Memories linger, like echoes in the air,
Each heartbeat a promise, tender and rare.

Through trials faced, and victories won,
Every lesson learned, a rising sun.
In quiet moments, we find our peace,
The wealth of love that will never cease.

So cherish each heartbeat, each breath we take,
In the garden of time, our dreams we'll make.
For in these moments, our riches gleam,
The wealth of life, a beautiful dream.

Treasures in Every Dawn

Each morning breaks with golden light,
A canvas bright, a new delight.
With gentle whispers, hope is born,
Promises wrapped in each new dawn.

A bird in flight sings sweet and clear,
Chasing away the shadows near.
In every dewdrop, dreams reside,
A treasure trove, the heart's guide.

The sun ascends, the world awakes,
With every heartbeat, life remakes.
Embrace the gift, let worries cease,
Find joy in movement, find your peace.

Blossoms of Abundance

Amidst the fields where flowers grow,
In vibrant hues, the colors show.
Each petal soft, a story spun,
In nature's dance, all hearts are one.

The breeze carries a sweet perfume,
In every blossom, life will bloom.
With open arms, we greet the day,
In nature's bounty, we will stay.

The harvest sings of thanks and cheer,
A song of love that draws us near.
For in this garden, we will find,
The joy of giving, hearts aligned.

A Tapestry of Triumph

Every struggle weaves a thread,
In the tapestry where dreams are fed.
Each victory, a vibrant hue,
Painting journeys of brave and true.

With courage stitched into our seams,
We rise through storms, we chase our dreams.
In unity, we stand so tall,
Together strong, we'll never fall.

The patterns blend, a sight so grand,
A work of art, by heart and hand.
Each woven tale, a lesson learned,
In this great fabric, love returns.

The Symphony of Success

In every note, a story flows,
A melody that gently grows.
Each chord a step along the way,
A symphony of bright ballet.

The rhythm pulses, hearts ignite,
Through joys and trials, we take flight.
With every beat, we find our song,
In harmony, we all belong.

The crescendo rises, spirits soar,
In unity, we seek to explore.
Together, in this dance we bask,
In the symphony, we are the task.

Celebrating the Overflow

In the garden, blooms align,
Colors dancing, hearts entwine.
Joy cascades, like rivers flow,
In this moment, love we sow.

With laughter bright, we cheer the day,
Together, find our own sweet way.
Each drop of joy, a treasure found,
In this space, our souls abound.

Underneath the endless sky,
Every dream begins to fly.
In abundance, we embrace,
Life's rich tapestry, our grace.

So here we stand, hands held tight,
Guided by the stars so bright.
In gratitude, we raise a toast,
To the overflow we cherish most.

Mosaics of Fulfillment

Fragments shimmer, colors blend,
Stories whisper, hearts transcend.
In every piece, a life unfolds,
Mosaics rich, and tales retold.

With each heartbeat, a vision grows,
Crafting paths that only love knows.
Shaped by hands both worn and wise,
The canvas blooms beneath the skies.

Patterns weave through night and day,
In unity, we find our way.
In every gap, hope finds a home,
Mosaics show we're never alone.

With colors bright, we paint our fate,
Each intertwined, intricate.
Together, strong, through thick and thin,
In this mosaic, we all win.

The Spirit of Growth

From tiny seeds, we rise and soar,
Nurtured by dreams, we crave for more.
In rain and sun, we stretch our wings,
Embracing all that each day brings.

Roots dig deep, and branches spread,
In every challenge, hope is fed.
Through storms that try to bend our frame,
The spirit grows in strength and flame.

In the stillness, lessons learned,
For every leaf, a heart must yearn.
The journey shapes who we will be,
In every moment, wild and free.

So tread the path, both wide and narrow,
In each challenge, find your arrow.
The spirit of growth will guide your way,
To brighter tomorrows, come what may.

Wings of Whimsy

With laughter light, we chase the breeze,
In every twist, we feel at ease.
Colors swirl in playful flight,
Wings of whimsy, pure delight.

In moonlit nights, we dance with stars,
Dreaming big and healing scars.
Imagination takes the lead,
In every heart, a secret seed.

Through winding paths, our spirits race,
Finding joy in every space.
With open hearts, we dare to roam,
In whims we find our truest home.

So let us fly, on dreams we ride,
With wings of whimsy, side by side.
In laughter's embrace, life's sweet song,
Together, we will always belong.

Joyful Pathways

In the morning light we roam,
With laughter echoing like a poem.
Each step we take, a dance of grace,
Finding joy in every place.

The trees above, they gently sway,
Whispering secrets of the day.
Nature's canvas, vast and bright,
Guiding us toward pure delight.

Hands intertwined, we walk as one,
Chasing shadows, chasing sun.
With every smile, the world expands,
Creating dreams with gentle hands.

As evening falls, the stars ignite,
Promising love and endless light.
In joyful pathways, hearts unite,
Embracing life, our spirits flight.

Seeds of Greatness

In every heart, a seed is sown,
Nurtured dreams waiting to be grown.
With care and love, they start to rise,
Reaching forth to touch the skies.

Through storms and shadows, they will bend,
For every journey has its end.
Yet rooted deep, they stand so strong,
A testament that they belong.

With patience, they will bloom and thrive,
Igniting passion, keeping hope alive.
Each step they take is filled with grace,
In every challenge, they find their place.

So nurture dreams with open hands,
Believe in greatness, in your plans.
For within you lies a golden key,
Unlock the doors to what can be.

The Radiant Quest

Through valleys deep, we seek the light,
With spirits bold, we rise in flight.
Every star guides us on our way,
Toward a dawn; we greet the day.

The mountains high, they call our name,
In whispers soft, they fuel our flame.
Though paths are steep, and shadows loom,
We chase the dreams that brightly bloom.

Together we forge a radiant path,
Finding courage in the aftermath.
In unity, our hearts will sing,
Embracing all that hope can bring.

So take my hand, let's journey far,
With every heartbeat, we're the star.
In this quest, we find our worth,
In the radiant quest on Earth.

Harvesting Happiness

In fields of gold, the sun shines bright,
Gathering joy, a pure delight.
Each moment savored, fresh and sweet,
Harvesting happiness, life is complete.

With laughter shared, we sow our days,
Watering dreams in countless ways.
The bounty rich, our hearts embrace,
Every smile adds to this space.

Through trials faced, we learn and grow,
In every lesson, love will flow.
Together we reap what we have sown,
Creating happiness, deeply grown.

So let us dance as seasons change,
Finding joy in every range.
For life's a gift, our hearts align,
In harvesting happiness, we shine.

Rich Roots

In the soil where dreams take flight,
Ancestors whisper through the night.
Their stories weave a tapestry,
Of strength and hope, a legacy.

Through trials faced, they stood so tall,
With love and courage, they gave their all.
Blessings flowing like a stream,
Rich roots nourish every dream.

In gardens lush, where shadows dance,
We honor them with every chance.
To nurture seeds of what they caused,
A harvest of love, forever paused.

Among the leaves, their spirits sing,
In every heart, their wisdom clings.
Connected deeply, we embrace,
The rich roots that time can't erase.

The Candle's Flame

A flicker in the silent dark,
It dances, it ignites a spark.
With gentle grace, it lights the gloom,
A beacon bright, dispelling doom.

The waxen body, melted slow,
Holds warmth within, a timeless glow.
In shadows deep, it finds its way,
A humble guide, both night and day.

In whispered thoughts, the flame reveals,
The quiet truth that love appeals.
As layers fade, the essence stays,
In glowing moments, in soft arrays.

Though flickering, it won't subside,
For every heart, there's light inside.
With every breath, let courage claim,
The power found in the candle's flame.

Liberated Laughter

In moments shared, a joyous sound,
With echoes bright, our hearts unbound.
Laughter bubbles, crisp and clear,
A melody that draws us near.

It dances freely in the air,
A song of joy beyond compare.
With every chuckle, worries flee,
A gift of light, pure harmony.

In playful jests, we shed our woes,
A freedom found where laughter grows.
With each shared grin, we rise above,
United in this art of love.

So let us laugh till daylight breaks,
In every heart, the joy awakes.
Liberated laughter, wild and bold,
A treasure worth more than gold.

Resonance of Riches

In every heart, a treasure lies,
Not wrapped in paper, nor in disguise.
A gentle touch, a steadfast hand,
Riches bloom in love's demand.

The laughter shared, the bonds that tie,
In simple moments, our spirits fly.
With open arms, we find our worth,
In every smile, in every birth.

Echoes of joy in every space,
Through whispers soft, we find our place.
Not measured by what we own or crave,
But in the kindness that we save.

So cherish these, the riches true,
The love we give, the love we pursue.
With every heartbeat, let's embrace,
The resonance of our shared grace.

Abundance in Bloom

In the garden where colors gleam,
Flowers dance in a sunlit dream.
Petals whisper secrets untold,
Nature's bounty, a sight to behold.

Joyful bees buzz, life swells,
Each blossom is magic that dwells.
From root to bloom, a wonderful thread,
Promises of harvest lying ahead.

Under the sky, the spirit sings,
A symphony found in simple things.
Every fragrance, a memory spun,
In the arms of abundance, we run.

Hope takes flight on a butterfly's wing,
Carrying tales of the love we bring.
In this garden, let hearts reside,
In ample joy, let us abide.

Echoes of Wealth

In the silence, gold softly calls,
Echoes of wealth in soft, quiet halls.
Dreams shimmer like stars in the night,
Guiding our steps towards hopeful light.

Moments cherished, treasures align,
In the tapestry woven, pure and fine.
Past and future blend in the now,
Grateful hearts with a humble vow.

Every smile, a gemstone rare,
Shared laughter fills the fragrant air.
Abundance flows from giving hands,
In these echoes, true fortune stands.

Awakened spirits roam free and bold,
In the warmth of connection, stories unfold.
We find our wealth in bonds we make,
As life's sweet melody begins to take.

The Golden Path Unfolds

Golden rays on a winding road,
Whispers of tales in the dew bestowed.
Each step forward, a promise renewing,
The path unfurls, brightly pursuing.

Through valleys deep and mountains high,
We walk together, just you and I.
Hand in hand, as the seasons change,
In the dance of life, we grow, we rearrange.

Footprints left in the soft, warm sand,
Crafting a journey so perfectly planned.
Every turn brings a moment's surprise,
Under the canvas of vast, open skies.

With every heartbeat, hope takes flight,
Guided by dreams that shine so bright.
On this golden path, our spirits soar,
Embracing the beauty of evermore.

Harvesting Dreams

Under the moon, where shadows play,
Dreams take root, they find their way.
In the quiet, intentions grow,
From tiny seeds to vibrant flow.

The fields of possibility stretch wide,
In the heart's garden, we take pride.
Sowing kindness, passion, and grace,
Nurturing hope in this sacred space.

With patience, we gather the fruits so bright,
In the golden dawn, bathed in light.
Each dream harvested, a story to tell,
In the bounty of life, all is well.

Together we weave a tapestry grand,
Of visions and wishes, united we stand.
In the act of dreaming, let's not delay,
For harvesting dreams is the soul's ballet.

The Canvas of Potential

A blank sheet waits for strokes of fate,
Colors blend, and dreams create.
Each line a step, each hue a chance,
Life's masterpiece in silent dance.

Visions rise in vibrant hues,
With every shade, a path ensues.
Aspire to weave the threads of time,
In every effort, a silent rhyme.

From dusk till dawn, the paint will flow,
Bold and soft, with rich undertow.
Embrace the unknown, let courage swell,
In this canvas, potential dwells.

So dream aloud, and take your brush,
Unfold your heart in the loveliest rush.
For within you lies a world unspun,
A canvas bright, where all is won.

The Allure of New Beginnings

In the hush of dawn, the world awakes,
Whispers of hope through the silence break.
A chance arrives, with every breath,
To rewrite stories, escape from dread.

The sun peeks through the curtains tight,
Casting shadows in the soft morning light.
Promises stir in the crisp, cool air,
A journey awaits, so tenderly rare.

With every heartbeat, a new pathway calls,
Embrace the climb, the rise, and falls.
For life unfolds in chapters bright,
Painted in colors of day and night.

So take a step, feel the thrill inside,
In this fresh start, let dreams abide.
With open arms and a heart that sings,
Welcome the joy that newness brings.

Portraits of Abundance

In fields of gold, the bounty thrives,
Each grain a story, each seed revives.
Nature's brush strokes a vibrant scene,
Portraits of abundance, lush and green.

From mountains high to rivers low,
Blessings abound that gently flow.
In laughter shared, and love's embrace,
We find the riches, our hearts' true place.

In every smile, a treasure found,
In every hand held, blessings abound.
The simplest moments, a wealth of grace,
In portraits painted, we find our space.

So gather close, and share the light,
In unity's glow, our spirits ignite.
For life's abundance is vast and wide,
In gratitude's warmth, we shall abide.

Blooming in the Sunlight

In gardens bright, where petals sway,
Colors burst forth, in vibrant display.
Each bloom a whisper, a tale to tell,
Of dreams that flourished, of hope that fell.

Underneath the golden rays,
Life awakens in wondrous ways.
With gentle winds, and skies so blue,
Nature dances, ever renewed.

Roots dig deep in fertile ground,
As blossoms open, beauty unbound.
In every fragrance, a story unfolds,
Of seasons passing, of warmth, and cold.

To bloom is to live, to reach for the light,
In the sun's embrace, all seems so right.
So let us thrive, in joy and in grace,
Blooming together, in this sacred space.

The Essence of Blooms

In gardens where the colors sway,
Petals whisper secrets of the day.
Softly they breathe the morning dew,
In vivid hues, their dreams shine through.

Beneath the sun, they stretch their arms,
Embracing warmth, their gentle charms.
Each blossom tells a tale of grace,
In every fold, the time they trace.

They dance with winds that softly sing,
Nature's joy on vibrant wings.
A symphony of life unfolds,
In every petal, love beholds.

The essence lies, both rich and pure,
In fleeting moments, hearts endure.
As seasons change, they fade away,
Yet in our hearts, their colors stay.

Luminous Pathways

The moonlit roads invite the night,
A dance of stars, a glorious sight.
Each step we take, so full of grace,
Guided by dreams we choose to chase.

Through forests deep, we wander far,
With whispers low and wishes star.
The air is thick with secrets told,
In luminous trails, our tales unfold.

We weave through paths of silver light,
Embracing shadows, chasing bright.
Each corner turned, a destiny,
In every heartbeat, we are free.

Together we stroll under the skies,
Painting our lives where wonder lies.
With hope as guide, we won't be lost,
In luminous pathways, love's the cost.

Bridges of Prosperity

Across the river, dreams unite,
Building bridges, hearts take flight.
With sturdy hands, we lay each stone,
Creating pathways, never alone.

In every span, a story told,
Of courage, faith, and visions bold.
Together we rise, hand in hand,
A tapestry of hope we've planned.

The echoes of laughter fill the air,
As friendships blossom, beyond compare.
In unity, our spirits soar,
With every step, we open doors.

These bridges crafted, strong and true,
A testament to what we can do.
For every challenge we embrace,
In bridges of prosperity, we find our place.

The Tides of Achievement

The ocean's waves, they rise and fall,
A rhythm steady, a beckoning call.
With every tide, a lesson learned,
In striving seas, our spirits turned.

We set our sails to chase the dreams,
Navigating life's flowing streams.
Through storms we journey, hearts set wide,
In the tides of achievement, we reside.

With courage fierce, we chart our way,
Forging ahead, come what may.
Each crest we ride, each trough we brave,
In every moment, we learn to save.

For glory lies not just in wins,
But in the growth that comes within.
So let us sail, forever free,
In the tides of achievement, joy shall be.

The Journey of Joy

In the dawn's gentle light, we arise,
With laughter and dreams, we reach for the skies.
Footsteps whisper softly on the path ahead,
Every moment cherished, no words left unsaid.

Through valleys of laughter, we dance along,
The rhythm of hearts beats a vibrant song.
Hand in hand we wander, no shadows cast,
Collecting each memory, making it last.

The sun paints our journey with colors so bright,
Guiding us gently through day and through night.
With joy as our compass, we navigate wide,
In the map of our hearts, love is our guide.

As stars twinkle down, our dreams take their flight,
In this journey of joy, we embrace pure light.
Together we travel, forever we'll roam,
Finding in each other, our true heart's home.

Endless Horizons

Beneath the vast sky, the world opens wide,
Endless horizons where secrets reside.
The ocean of dreams calls, a whisper so clear,
Inviting our spirits to dance without fear.

Horizons expanding with each step we take,
The promise of wonders, a path we will make.
Mountains of courage rise high in the east,
A banquet of beauty, life's grandest feast.

With every sunrise, new stories will bloom,
The canvas of life, filled with joy, never gloom.
Together we chase what the future might bring,
In the song of the winds, our hearts learn to sing.

Through valleys of passion and rivers of hope,
We journey together, beneath stars that elope.
Endless horizons await our embrace,
With love in our hearts, we find our own place.

Threads of Delight

In a tapestry woven, each thread shines bright,
Moments of laughter, in colors of light.
A stitch of togetherness, soft and so warm,
We gather the joys, reflecting life's charm.

Each day we weave dreams, new stories to tell,
In the fabric of friendship, we flourish and swell.
With needles of kindness, we craft and we mend,
Creating a quilt, where the echoes transcend.

Through textures of life, we glide with such grace,
Finding beauty in chaos, our hearts interlace.
In the threads of delight, we discover our way,
Woven in love, we brighten each day.

Embracing the moments, both simple and sweet,
In the circle of laughter, our lives are complete.
Threads of delight bind us, a radiant chain,
Together forever, through joy and through pain.

Fragrant Futures

In gardens of hope, where blossoms ignite,
Fragrant futures bloom, as day turns to night.
Petals of promise, unfurling with grace,
Whispers of potential in each sacred space.

The scent of adventure fills the warm air,
Inviting our dreams to blossom and dare.
With every new dawn, we plant seeds of trust,
In the soil of our hearts, grow strong and robust.

Through the fragrance of kindness, we'll navigate fate,
In this dance of tomorrow, we cultivate.
With laughter like dew on each tender leaf,
We tend to our futures, embracing belief.

As the sun paints the skies in soft pastel hues,
We gather the moments, both old and new.
Fragrant futures calling, we rise, we aspire,
In this garden of life, we grow ever higher.

Milton Keynes UK
Ingram Content Group UK Ltd.
UKHW022359051024
449245UK00006B/45